Enabling
the
Disabled

 **My Personal Story**

by

D HEATHER GRAHAM

ISBN: 978-1-910719-43-5

Published for D Heather Graham by
Verité CM Limited,
Unit 2, Martlets Way, Goring Business Park,
Goring-by-Sea, West Sussex BN12 4HF

+44 (0) 1903 241975
email: enquiries@veritecm.com
Web: www.veritecm.com

British Library Cataloguing Data

A catalogue record of this book is available from The British Library

Design and Typesetting by Verité CM Ltd

Printed in England

Introduction

I have spent over half a century in the caring professions: as a nurse, special needs teacher, care assistant and home manager. I started as an ophthalmic nurse in 1958 and finally retired from work in 2013. My career has involved working with many of what we now call "client groups": eye patients, the physically and mentally handicapped and the elderly. It is indeed a reflection of the change I have experienced that the very words used to describe the cared for have changed. A case in point is the word "spastic", which is no longer used to describe people with cerebral palsy, although at one time it was non-pejorative term derived from the Greek (via Latin) "spastikos", meaning "tugging". It was only as recently as 1994 that the Spastics Society was renamed Scope (but the term is still used in the scientific literature). Less provocative is the term "mental handicap", but even that has been replaced by the phrase "people with (severe) learning difficulties".

This book started out as a memoir for family and friends, but I decided that it would be interesting for those working in the field and the families of those affected by the conditions discussed to have a first-hand account of someone working on the frontline. What I can contribute is the long perspective of fifty years and a diversity of experience. The latter was product of circumstance. My husband – Douglas – is a retired Methodist minister. The Methodist Church has a system whereby ministers are moved every five years or so, with the result that we relocated more often than most people (perhaps only service families are more frequent movers). Since our marriage in 1961 we have lived in eight towns, from the Lancashire coast to the south coast, with stops along the way in Bedfordshire, Yorkshire, Buckinghamshire, Kent, Sussex and Kent (again). While moving has been a strain I have gained enormously from the number of people I have got to know.

While my attitudes to disability have been shaped by my Christian beliefs this book is written for anybody interested in the topic, whether or not you share those beliefs.

Please note that all names of those under my care have been changed.

D Heather Graham
January 2017

Acknowledgements

This book is dedicated to my family. To my husband, Rev Douglas Graham, who has shown immense patience and encouragement and also my sons, Nigel, Allistair and Paul who in the first place encouraged me to put pen to paper of my experiences working with disabled and vulnerable people.

My special thanks goes to our son Dr Paul Graham, who has proof-read the book and made helpful suggestion on setting it out. Without him I doubt this book would have been produced.

Thanks to them all,

Heather

Chapter 1:

 Changing Attitudes

*"'Cursed be anyone who misleads a blind man
on the road.' And all the people shall say, 'Amen.'"*
Deuteronomy 27:18

I was born in Dublin in 1941, on the night Germans accidently bombed the city, despite Ireland's neutrality. Brought up in the suburb of Clontarf, which abuts onto the Bull Wall and whose most famous resident was Bram Stoker, author of Dracula, my family were devout Protestants. My father – Fred – had been brought up Plymouth Brethren, but had become a Baptist. My background played an important part in my motivation and I return to this in the last chapter, but I want to start by reflecting on how attitudes to disability have changed over the period of my career.

We left Ireland in 1946, when my father got a job with Good Year Tyres in Wolverhampton in the West Midlands. I didn't shine academically and unlike my two sisters, failed my 11-plus exam for entry to the local grammar school. While I eventually got a job at the Eye Infirmary there were some further disappointments on the way. I went for interview to train as a house parent for the National Children's Home in Hertfordshire, but wasn't successful. I'd have loved the job and knew I would be good at it, as I adored children. Compensation did come on my fifteenth birthday in the form of a job as nanny to three children of a local Methodist minister.

I started aged seventeen at the Eye Infirmary. Fortunately, at that time O-Levels were not required for entry to nursing (how times have changed; nursing is becoming a graduate-level occupation). What was required was to be resident in the nurses' home, which suited me fine, as I, like many young people, was keen to leave home. In 1957 the National Health Service (NHS) was just ten years old and very different to the NHS of today. I was never addressed by my Christian name – it was always Cochran (my maiden name). We all wore knee length dresses, while the – few – male nurses had a uniform consisting of white trousers and a white top. The female nurses had a white apron over their dresses, with the top bib part pinned to the dress on the inside of the apron so the pins weren't showing and we all wore starched caps and had to have our hair tied back.

We had to respect the senior nurses. A junior nurse would not go through a door in front of a nurse slightly senior to her. If I went into the dining-room and was the junior nurse in there I had to watch out for any of the sisters getting up to leave the dining room. I would have to go and open the door for her whether or not I had finished my meal.

We had to have everything prepared for the rounds. In order for the doctors to perform the various procedures on the wards the trollies must be laid up. They had to be cleaned with carbolic swabs, which were held with forceps. Sterile towels, along with such things as galley pots, were then placed on the trollies. All the instruments had to be sterilised in boiling water. Nurses had to know which instruments were required. These days everything comes in sterile packs that are opened as needed. Again, we had to open and close doors for the doctors.

Watching period TV nursing programmes, such as 'Call the Midwife', is quite interesting. It is set in the late 1950s and early 1960s and is a relatively accurate portrayal of the time, although it perhaps downplays the level of deference required of junior nurses.

There were no computers. Everything was written by hand. And filed. Patients had a clipboard on the end of their bed containing various notes like "temperature, pulse and respiration records" (TPR).

We used to see a lot of Matron at the eye infirmary as it was a small hospital. She was very approachable. Sister Tutor was the one to keep a watch out for as she could do a ward round at any time. I got caught by her one time sitting on a patient's bed chatting to him. This was regarded as very unprofessional; I should have stood to talk to the patient.

At the much larger Royal General Hospital Wolverhampton – to which I transferred from the Eye Infirmary – the only time I saw the matron was on my first day. The atmosphere was quite different, but still very strict. There was, however, less of the door-opening type of behaviour as meals were canteen style. I enjoyed night duty (8 pm-8 am), which was usually a three-month stretch of four nights on duty, and three nights off.

Medical treatments have changed hugely over the years. An example is a cataract operation. When I was doing ophthalmic nursing in the late 1950s we nursed people who had cataract operations for about two weeks, as they weren't allowed to strain. They had a pad on their eye for the best part of those two weeks. Now the operation takes about twenty minutes and you go home the same day. The same applies to retinal detachments. If it was a top detachment the person lay in bed for weeks with the end of the bed propped up. If it was a bottom detachment they sat up in bed for longer. Now it is treated by laser, and the patient goes home the same day. There weren't knee or hip replacements or organ transplant operations then.

Married in 1961 most of the 1960s was taken up with having children. We moved to South Yorkshire in 1970 and when my youngest son began school in 1971 I again started looking for full-time work and found it as a classroom assistant at a special school for physically disabled children. Some history is helpful here. Under the famous 1944 Education Act children were categorized by their "special educational needs". This would begin to change in the late 1970s, with the Warnock Report (1978), which was followed by the 1981 Education Act. That Act introduced the idea of special educational needs (SEN) and of SEN "statements". Crucially, it also advanced the notion of an "integrative" – later termed "inclusive" – approach, based on common educational goals for all children irrespective of (dis)ability: independence, enjoyment and understanding. The practical effect was to close many special schools and educate children in mainstream ones, although unfortunately, very little money was set aside to implement these changes.[1] It is significant that in researching this book I found it difficult to locate my former school on google maps, although I did eventually work out that it had been converted to a regular primary school.

In the early 1970s several children still wore heavy calipers, but they weren't to wear them all day. The children were exercised in the calipers for short periods. We would check they hadn't any chafing from wearing these cumbersome things. While calipers are still used today they are much more sophisticated and better adapted to the needs of users.

---

[1] *Special Educational Needs: Third Report of the Session, 2005-6, House of Commons: www.publications.parliament.uk/pa/cm200506/cmselect/cmeduski/478/478i.pdf. Accessed 10/04/16.*

I had charge of eighteen in my group, which was a little overwhelming. Many were in their 30s and 40s and had missed out on any formal education. It was only in 1972 that the law required all children to be educated. I began teaching, but it was not ordinary teaching. Reading was sight recognition with flash cards. Education prior to the 1970s was so patchy that older people often couldn't distinguish male and female toilets. Obviously, this kind of thing severely restricted the ability to live anything approaching an independent life.

As suggested earlier, the 1978 Warnock Report re-examined the situation of people with special needs. Parallel to this – and starting in the early 1960s – there was a move to close large institutions and move people into smaller units and "into the community"; this was later dubbed, often with pejorative overtones, "care in the community". Sometimes institutions were closed down for dubious reasons, such as a way of realising the land value for housing. But there were also good motives behind the policy. Until that time many people suffering from disabilities such as tuberculosis (TB), polio, mental illness and physical impairments were admitted to isolated institutions. A large number of these institutions were appalling, with poor sanitation, mental and physical abuse, and with patients often isolated from family and friends and from the community. They slept in big dormitories and this added to the person's problems.

The generations that had been through these institutions faced challenges in adjusting. The effects were still being felt in the late 1990s. At that time I worked in a residential home in Kent. One particular gentleman in his 50s had been, from early childhood, in a very large institution for people with learning difficulties and he moved to this smaller, more homely residential home. He took years to adjust. Sleeping in a single room frightened him; it was too quiet at night and he often came downstairs and slept on the settee so he could hear the night staff moving around. He carried a plastic carrier bag with him wherever he went. In it were his cutlery, toothbrush and toothpaste, face flannel, towel and toilet roll. In the big institution such things were used by other residents, so he kept them close to his person. Also he gulped down his meals faster than anyone else; again he had been used to others stealing his food if he paused for a minute. At first, it was impossible for any of our staff to break these habits. But he did develop in confidence. He learnt to chat with many people and after much training and risk assessment he would go on his own to the shop near the home, for his sweets and biscuits.

The big changes I experienced over my career can be summarised as the move to a more person-centred approach to disability. There was a move away from big institutions to trying to integrate disabled people into the community. Language also changed, with a greater sensitivity in the words used to describe different types of disability.

Chapter 2:

What is Disability?

*"He said also to the man who had invited him,
'When you give a dinner or a banquet, do not invite
your friends or your brothers or your relatives or rich
neighbours, lest they also invite you in return and you
be repaid. But when you give a feast, invite the poor,
the crippled, the lame, the blind'".* Luke 14:12-13.

Disability is an umbrella term for impairments of activity and participation, and for restrictions in everyday life. The term "disability" means different things to different people, and as I suggested in chapter 1 its meaning has changed over time. Arguably, because I wear glasses and have two hearing aids I am disabled. They are the first things on in the mornings and last things off at night and without them I would find it hard to function. Disability isn't necessarily about being in a wheelchair. Disability can include blindness, deafness, and difficulty in walking, speaking, standing or sitting up or in understanding the world around you.

Some people are born with disabilities such as Downs' syndrome and cerebral palsy. Others develop disabilities in later life. These might include, for example, epilepsy, Parkinson's disease, muscular dystrophy, multiple sclerosis and various types of mental illness. Downs syndrome, cerebral palsy and some muscular conditions, such as spina bifida, occur in the womb or at birth. These are not contagious, and are usually permanent, affecting posture, speech, movement and behaviour. Millions of people worldwide have some disability, which can be a physical, emotional or mental handicap.

There is still a lot of discrimination towards disabled people, both in and out of the workplace. But disability can cause not just discrimination, but also health and social care issues, as well as depression, sleep disorder and bullying. People with learning difficulties are particularly susceptible to these problems, through lack of understanding. This is especially true of autistic people, who look "normal", but behave in an unusual way. People with Downs' syndrome appear noticeably different and they can behave like a person with autism, but there is a greater degree of understanding for their behaviour, because their condition is more evident.

There is often a serious underestimation of the capacity of disabled people to do well in life. The Paralympics has shown what disabled people are capable of in terms of sporting excellence, but in more mundane settings disability is no bar to achievement and social integration. For example, a blind person can live in his or her own home, with some extra help where needed.

Disabled people can be extremely gifted at arts and crafts. I know a lady who had a brain haemorrhage, and can only use one hand and yet does the most amazingly intricate mosaics, and can also paint. Other people are good potters, knitters and needle-workers. I have worked with a totally blind man who, like the woman mentioned above, does wonderful mosaics. He is given differently coloured tiles and places them in the defined area, which has been shaped with either plasticine or blue-tac, and can then be moved to shape the next area. A woman in a wheelchair – having broken her back in a riding accident – attends a day centre as a volunteer and teaches cooking to the clients.

In Chapter 3 I explain my practical experience in educating disabled people and show what I have found to be possible. But in the rest of this chapter I want to outline specific types of disability that I have experienced in my career (I must stress that I am no expert in any of the following conditions):

> • **Cerebral palsy** is an umbrella terms for a condition that causes disabilities in bodily movement. The term "cerebral" refers to the brain. It is a permanent condition but a lot can be done to improve movement and posture. The palsy can be accompanied by a disturbance of understanding (cognition), communication, perception and sensation. It also can give rise to epilepsy. Not all these symptoms are present in a person with cerebral palsy. It is the most common of all childhood disabilities, affecting around 3 in every one thousand live births. There are different kinds of palsy. Figures from the United States (the UK won't be much different) are: spastic 76.9%; dyskinetic 2.6%; hypotonic 2.6%; ataxic 2.4%; other types 15.4%.[2]

> • **Athetoid cerebral palsy** is a relatively rare condition within the larger condition of cerebral palsy. It is caused by damage to the cerebellum or basal ganglia areas of the brain and affects the processing of coordination and physical balance. The child may develop involuntary movements in their facial muscles, arms

---

[2] *www.cerebralpalsy.org/about-cerebral-palsy/prevalence-and-incidence.*

and body. These involuntary movements can interfere with speaking, feeding, and the reaching out for, and grasping of, objects. Emotional stress can exacerbate these movements, while sleep can ameliorate them. Children often wear specially designed braces.

• **Autism** is a severe development disorder which manifests itself at birth or within the first two or three years. Children with autism look normal in appearance but display puzzling and sometimes disturbing behaviour. Some children are diagnosed with Pervasive Development Disorder (PDD), which is a less severe form of autism.

Autism is a brain condition which impairs social interaction and communication, and can cause repetitive behaviour. The younger the child is diagnosed the earlier treatment can begin and the better the outcome for the child. Early intervention increases the likelihood he or she can attend a normal school and live a semi-independent life in the community. A very good book on the subject is Temple Grandin, *The Autistic Brain*. She understands the complexities of autism as she is herself autistic, but has learnt to cope with the condition.

Some autistic people are described as 'high functioning', meaning that they have an IQ above 70. There are some cases where an autistic person can show extremely high skills, especially in the spatio-visual field. There are celebrated cases of this in popular culture.

• **Osteogenesis Imperfecta** (Brittle Bone Syndrome) is usually a hereditary disease. It reveals itself as a deficiency in bone formation and connective tissues, rendering the bones fragile. Babies can suffer multiple fractures and die in infancy. Less severely affected children can often reach adulthood with fewer fractures; what factures are suffered tend to be in the legs. The sclera – white of the eyes – can have a bluish hue; indeed, in the absence of less severe symptoms this can be a sign of the condition.

• **Downs Syndrome** is named after the physician – John Langdon Down – who identified it. Downs Syndrome causes mild to moderate learning difficulties. It results from a chromosomal disorder, where there is a full or partial third copy of chromosome 21.

Those with Downs almost always have physical and intellectual impairments. They often have the mental age of an 8- or 9-year-old. Typically they have a poor immune function and are at increased risk for a range of health problems such as heart problems, epilepsy, leukemia and thyroid disease.

• **Epilepsy** is often associated with damage to the brain and is both a condition in itself and a symptom of other conditions, such as Downs Syndrome. Epileptic seizures are a sign of brain damage, although they may not be experienced until many years after the damage has occurred. While epilepsy is usually the result of brain damage, repeated seizures can themselves damage the brain and over time worsen a person's disability.

Given there is no specific test for epilepsy it can be difficult to diagnose. Often diagnosis is based on the affected person describing the attacks or on eye-witness accounts. Diagnosing epilepsy in a person with learning difficulties is very difficult as unusual physical movements can be characteristics of other disabilities. In addition, a person with severe learning difficulties can find it hard to communicate his or her experiences

• **Fragile X Syndrome** (FXS) is a recessive condition, meaning that both parents normally have to carry two copies of the gene (or allele) for their child to be affected.

FXS is the most common cause of autism or autistic-like behaviour and can impair speech, memory and physical balance. Children with FXS have many behavioural characteristics. They are often described as sweet and lovable, with a good sense of humour. However, they can also be impulsive and suffer from Attention Deficit Hyperactive Disorder (ADHD). This is particularly the case with boys who have FXS; girls may be less hyperactive but still have the symptoms of Attention Deficit Disorder (ADD).

Many boys have peculiar sensory problems and suffer anxiety, which is often the result of unusual sensitivity to sound or light. Sufferers can react badly to changes in routine, to fire drills and to travel. Crowds can be especially stressful. Tantrums can result. With training and loving discipline from everyone involved these problems can be overcome.

• **Friedrich's Ataxia** is an inherited condition which affects the nervous system and causes muscular weakness. It can also affect speech and is associated with heart disease. Friedrich's Ataxia causes the degeneration of nerve tissues and of the nerves of the spinal cord that control muscle movement in the arms and legs.

Symptoms usually begin in childhood, but can appear in infancy. Walking is often the first symptom something is wrong, but then arm movements and the rest of the body can be affected. Curvature of the spine eventually develops. Other symptoms can be chest pains and breathlessness. Heart problems are also associated with the condition.

Doctors diagnose Friedrich's Ataxia through careful examination, including a consultation of the person's medical history. The condition can go into remission for periods of five or ten years, or even longer. It can affect both sexes.

• **Haemophilia** is a rare – normally inherited – blood condition in which the blood doesn't clot. Sufferers have little or no clotting mechanism. Haemophiliacs may bleed for a long time after an injury. They may bleed internally, especially around their knees, ankles and elbows. The bleeding can damage their organs and tissues and may be life-threatening.

• **Huntington's Disease** is an inherited brain disorder named after George Huntington. It causes physical and mental changes and is often identified by involuntary, jerky movements that develop gradually in the later stages of the illness.

• **Myotonic Dystrophy** causes muscle weakness and wasting. It is an inherited condition. While very variable in its effects there are some common features. The muscles of the face are frequently affected, as is the jaw and neck; leg and thigh muscles less commonly so. Muscle stiffness (or Myotonia) is a characteristic. People with myotonic dystrophy often have difficulty releasing a hand grip. Time of onset varies but can be anywhere from birth to old age. Associated problems are tiredness, cataracts, constipation, infertility in males, disturbance in heart rhythm, diabetes, irregular periods in females and learning difficulties in children.

Each of these conditions is distinctive and so the term "disability" covers a huge range of syndromes, each with its own challenges. This sheer variety means those working with disabled people have to be versatile. In a sense they must be both generalists and specialists: adept at working with people with very different needs – often in the same home and on the same day – but also specialists, capable of understanding particular vulnerabilities.

Chapter 3:

 Overcoming Disability

"So that the crowd wondered, when they saw the mute speaking, the crippled healthy, the lame walking, and the blind seeing. And they glorified the God of Israel".
Matthew 15:31.

Among the things I have learnt during my career are that you have to be flexible and adapt to the circumstances and needs of individuals; you don't learn by reading books – although it is important to take on board the latest research. In this chapter I describe how I have discovered ways of helping people overcome their limitations.

I remember eight year old Tim, who suffered from brittle bone syndrome. Tim loved playing football on our large playing field. I was expecting cracked or broken bones. His mother put in writing her permission for Tim to play whatever games he wished, so he could lead as normal a life as possible. To my knowledge Tim was never rushed to hospital with broken bones.

There were also twin sisters Hidie and Sarah, both were born with cerebral palsy, both walked with Zimmer frames to secure their balance. Part of my job was to encourage them to take a few steps without their Zimmers. To our delight, Hidie gained confidence and started taking a few steps unaided before ending up in a heap on the floor or catching hold of me or another staff member. Sarah took longer, but was determined to copy her sister, and would play copycat.

Daniel and Gabriel were teenage lads. Both suffered from haemophilia. This is where, if cut or bruised, they bleed excessively, which can be life-threatening. On playground duty the staff's hearts missed beats as these two wheelchair bound young men would line up at each end of the concrete playground, then on their back wheels raced towards each other at a terrific rate – and as in the game of "chicken" – looked to be heading for each other, but missed at the last minute by either stopping or passing the other. They were normal teenage lads, living life to the full, as they knew it, and needed to be treated and trusted as such.

All of these are cases where staff had to take risks if their "clients" were to develop self-confidence or simply enjoy life in the same way as other children or young people. But another aspect of "enabling the disabled" involves a degree of either serendipity or conscious subterfuge.

Andrew comes to mind. He could neither walk nor talk and constantly shook his head, which was a symptom of athetoid dyskinesia. Trying to feed Andrew was a challenge, especially as he didn't like savoury food. One day the teacher was serving lunch from the hot trolley, thinking she was pouring fish sauce on Andrew's fish, she mistakenly poured custard on it. He loved it, and after that neither we nor his parents had problems feeding Andrew so long as we sprinkled a little sugar on his savoury meals.

Another case is that of eight year old Tina. After moving from Yorkshire to Buckinghamshire in the mid-1970s I took up a post in a school for children with "dual handicaps" – learning and physical. We were lucky to be close to a very good, and newly opened, Olympic-size swimming pool as well as a hydrotherapy pool at the school. I have always loved swimming and it was great to use it as part of the teaching programme. Swimming is very important in building confidence and along with other members of the school staff I became a swimming instructor. We taught numerous children to swim. In the hydrotherapy pool I learnt to play what I called the waiting game. Tina went in the pool twice a week, but she was very nervous and clung tightly to the bar. She did all the leg swimming movements and after many months she would cautiously take one hand off the bar, but no way would she take both off at the same time. Tina wasn't nervous about getting her face wet and she loved blowing bubbles. So how could we encourage her to let go of the bar?

She had a watch which didn't work; that didn't matter, as it was her favourite item, and she always wore it. We found in a junk shop an almost identical watch. After nearly two years of trying every conceivable trick to get Tina to let go of the bar we dropped the junk shop watch into the pool in front of her. She immediately let go of the bar and dived for the watch, thinking it was hers. There was no stopping her after that. Children who had learnt to swim would be taken each week to the local 50 metre one. Six months after Tina began swimming she was going to this Olympic-size pool. About this time the school organised a gala, with spectators made up of parents and friends. Tina won a number of trophies.

Swimming has been one of the most enjoyable activities which I have undertaken with those under my care and along with basic instructor certificates I acquired various qualifications in life-saving. One summer we took a group from the school on holiday to Suffolk and hired three self-catering apartments in the holiday complex. We were in the swimming pool and one of our young people who could swim a little got out of her depth and as I was on the side of the pool watching her I immediately dived in to get her to shallower water. The lifeguard was a somewhat amazed at my speed and reaction. I explained to him I had done life-saving and he in turn gave me free access to the Turkish bath which I had never experienced before, which was great.

After I had worked at the school for two years, the education authority thought it a good idea to start a further education group, which meant sixteen year old young people would stay on to nineteen instead of leaving and going to the local day centre. A teacher was appointed. The teacher needed a teaching assistant. I was appointed from five who were interviewed.

The group began with four young people: Janet, Lora, Megan and Thomas. We got them involved in various projects outside the school, such as cooking at the local Further Education College, alongside mature students. We had to use public transport, which was good training for our students, but quite inconvenient from the time aspect. I learnt to drive the school minibus; because they were young people in a care situation I was required to take a driving test. I quickly learnt that there were specific techniques to driving a minibus, which had a hydraulic tailgate. I failed the first test. The town was very hilly and some roads had quite extreme gradients. When I was driving a heavy vehicle down a hill, I needed to change to a low gear before descending the hill. I hadn't done this in the first test.

We taught the group new ways of being independent, such as travel training. None of them had experienced this before. One day a week they joined O-Level students at another FE College to learn home decorating: painting, papering, stenciling, grouting and many other aspects of decorating. The experience was good for our students and for the college students. Many friends were made.

We enrolled the group on the Duke of Edinburgh Scheme, which really stretched them – and us. All gained bronze and some gained silver awards.

There were some scary moments. The group visited a local museum, which was on three floors. Returning to the ground floor, we were confronted by one of our group – Thomas – who panicked coming down the stairs. He wouldn't move and there were no lifts in the building. The only way we could get him down was to blindfold him. Three-quarters of an hour later we reached the ground floor with Thomas coming down backwards, which is not the most dignified way to descend a flight of stairs. The museum staff assisted us by closing the museum until we were safely down. We worked with him around his fear and gradually won the battle.

Life skills are an important part of dealing with disability and they can be particularly challenging with older people. After moving to Kent in 1980 I started working at a day centre with a more mixed age range. Colin, a 50 year old man, lived with his 80 year old mother, who was finding it difficult coping with him. Colin's hygiene was off-putting. I felt I could teach him to wash and iron at the day centre. I visited his home to assess how he might be able to manage and discovered his mother had a twin tub washing machine very like the one we had in the day centre training kitchen. Colin brought in his change of clothes every day and learnt to wash and dry them. He then learnt to iron them. This took a while, but he eventually succeeded. The only mistake he made was that he ironed a pair of nylon socks with too hot an iron.

He and his mother only had a shower as their previous owners had removed the bath. Neither knew how to work the shower. This was a new skill they both learnt through the help of the day centre.

I was concerned that Colin had no knowledge of cooking simple meals, having gone home on one occasion to find his mother ill in bed. He hadn't had anything to eat or drink all weekend. I started at the day centre what I called 'Emergency Cooking' with Colin and other clients. Many of them learnt to open tins, a skill they had never been taught, as parents feared they would cut themselves. We started with simple ideas such as making beans on toast or spaghetti or boiling an egg. As Clive and the other clients gained confidence by learning some of these everyday tasks we also witnessed personalities blossom and challenging behaviour fade.

I used this experience a decade later when I became manager of a home in South East London (of which more later). The home was actually a series of what had been ordinary houses. A young man who had been having respite care for some time in Number 1 house was going to move into Number 3 with the other young men. Furniture had already been bought, but as the house had to be fitted out with kitchenware, such as crockery and utensils, I worked for the first couple of months in the main house which enabled me to get to know the young men I would be working with. This gave me and my line manager John time to buy all the essentials for the house. These were exciting days. When we moved in we had four full time staff, two weekend staff and a volunteer. I should mention here that the Number 4 house was quite derelict and was used as a storehouse while Number 5 house was reserved for volunteer staff who were from abroad and came to gain work experience for a year. They were all a great help. One of our weekend staff was Japanese and had come as a volunteer but had been offered a permanent job.

I decided that I would run the house as an independent training home for the residents. They all had to learn to cook, wash, iron, hoover, clean their rooms, and so on. And they also learnt to shop. I made a lot of flash cards. One day when we got to the supermarket I gave two of the young people three flash cards each to go around and collect their items and bring them back to the trolley where I was waiting. Young Simon, who had very poor speech, came back with a huge grin on his face; he had been to the delicatessen and showed the assistant the card and she cut him a decent sized piece of cheese. He was delighted.

Every year we took them on holiday to Haven Holiday camps. The first one was in Prestatyn (North Wales). At night the young people enjoyed the disco and were always first up on the dance floor. On one of these holidays we encountered some teenagers making fun of our young lads; while dancing I approached them and explained that our young men were no different to themselves in a lot of ways, except they had a disability. One of the parents of the group I was talking to wondered what I was saying to them so I explained. For the rest of the week these teenagers became best of friends with our lads and even after we returned home corresponded with them.

Another holiday we had was on Corfu. By this time our home had admitted two more young men. We took all six lads and six staff on holiday. We stayed in three self-catering chalets. One of the young men – Matt – caused a bit of a problem at the airport on the return journey. He sat on the floor of the airport waiting area and wouldn't move when we were expected to board our plane. We wondered what to do, and so one of the carers told the rest of us to board so Matt would see us all disappear. At the last minute Matt got up and ran to the plane. We were all relieved.

All our lads attended the local college. The college ran special training for people with learning disabilities; this was a three year course. I talked to John my line manager about what we would do with the young people when they had to leave college. As sometime previously the family in Number 2 had been rehoused elsewhere the property was now empty and being refurbished. I wondered if we could use it as a day centre. Based on my experience in Kent I felt it could work. So John and I visited various day centres to see some of the things on offer. In 1999 the day centre in Number 2 was officially opened. We appointed three new staff, including myself, to oversee the start of the project. Having the day centre gave our young people something to do and somewhere to go each day. To this day it is still going strong.

I was a great encourager of getting disabled people – particularly younger people – to join leisure activities and groups such as dance and drama, keep fit groups exercising to music, to swim and to practice relaxation techniques. These were means to build confidence and make friends. I have watched and (sometimes) joined in with them playing volleyball, football, table tennis, cricket, croquet, darts and snooker. People who weren't able to move easily could play board games such as scrabble, backgammon and Ludo. Many also enjoyed Karaoke. I encouraged able-bodied people to volunteer to compete against our residents which proved valuable to both parties. Lasting friendships were established.

Some of the disabled people joined a sailing club and one or two became crew on the Lord Nelson sailing ship, where they had to work by helping to sail the ship. They took holidays of either a few days or week in which they were joined by an able-bodied person, who assisted them in the various tasks involved in sailing the boat.

One weekend we took a group of young people on a boat trip down the Thames. One of the staff had experience of sailing and taught us how to steer the boat. We moored the boat and sat on a grassy bank on the Windsor Castle estate. When we got back to the boat we couldn't move it, so two of the staff had to enter the shallow water and push it into deeper water, while the staff on the boat had quickly to pull them into the boat or else it would have been carried out by the current without them.

Some of the disabled people enjoyed the artificial ski and tobogganing club. With special equipment they could enjoy the thrill of the ski slope.

Another attraction was the mobile library, which enabled people with disabilities to borrow books and videos. I encouraged our people to go to the library to see what was on offer. Importantly, the library staff got to know them.

Helping disabled people is often about being imaginative in finding a solution. One person I worked with suffered from cerebral palsy. She was quite intelligent and wanted to use her typewriter but her hand movement wouldn't allow her to do this. A friend of her family came up with the idea of making a board and screwing two rowing boat rowlocks into the board. By then screwing the board to a table she could put her wrists in the rowlocks and type. She used to type the home's newsletter a couple of times a year.

Chapter 4:

 Challenges

*"Blessed are those who mourn,
for they shall be comforted."* Matthew 5:4

In this chapter I want to explore a number of challenges facing disabled people, those who work with and care for disabled people, and society at large: frustration and aggression; sex and marriage; death and bereavement; abuse.

....

Disabled people have the same emotions as anyone else. However, these can be heightened by a lack of self-control and by being unable to do what they want to do. Frustration due to an inability to do something may be more intense for a physically handicapped person, because they are more conscious of their disability and it can be even more acute if the disability is acquired – for example, if the person has suffered an accident or developed a degenerative condition.

Matt suffered from Fragile X Syndrome. He could become frustrated and aggressive, although never violent. If he was frustrated, by not having his own way, he would lie down on the floor or, if in town, on the ground. Such episodes could last three-quarters of an hour. When I first encountered this – something of which I had been warned – I told him kindly but firmly to get up. This brought a response from shoppers, who tried to help. I politely asked them to leave him alone. I told him I was going home and he would have to walk home by himself. His response was immediately to get up. He never did it again with me, but he did try it on with other staff. But forewarned they all took the same approach, and that helped Matt with his frustration.

We did work to understand his aggression. If he lost at Ludo, dominoes or card games Matt would get angry. These outbursts had to be addressed. We explained to him that he wouldn't always win.

Another young person I worked with, who had Downs Syndrome, could become very frustrated, particularly if he wasn't 'Top Dog' as the saying goes. We were aware of his ability for acting. Although he didn't do speech parts, he played lead roles in plays at his local college. He was also an excellent dancer. This counteracted his frustration and aggression.

It always amused me how Downs syndrome people loved attention. Liam would regularly be taken swimming. On one occasion he feigned an epileptic fit in the pool. Convincing both the care worker and the life-guard he was brought home. After it was suggested he go and have a rest Liam had the care worker running around, bringing him drinks and things to eat. When my deputy officer came on duty later that day, asking where Liam was she was told he'd had a fit in the pool, to which she replied he didn't have fits and was up to his old tricks of attention-seeking. She told him to get up and apologise, which he reluctantly did.

....

Having pets can be hugely beneficial, although not without risks should something happen to them. When I first became manager of the care home in South East London my deputy asked the young people if they would like a pet; after discussion they decided a cat would be the easiest to look after and more friendly than a caged pet. We took the young people to a local cattery and they fell in love with a ginger cat called Barkus. He had been brought to the cattery to be re-housed by someone who couldn't cope with a pet. The young people fought over who would feed her. So we set up a rota.

In the evening, while watching TV, they would curl up on the sofa, cuddling and stroking Barkus. Each of the residents paid weekly into a fund for her food and – if ever required – vet's fees. Before we collected Barkus we had her tagged and looked over by a vet.

After about a year Barkus vanished. We searched everywhere for her, asked neighbours and even informed the police, in case she had been killed on the road. But we didn't hear anything. We wondered whether she had been stolen. The young people were desperately upset – as were the staff. The young people decided they didn't want another pet cat, in case the same thing happened again.

At various places I have worked 'Pets as Therapy' (PAT) has been employed. Trained dogs were brought in by a handler. They were a calming influence. PAT is used in lots of situations, including in schools and colleges to relieve examination stress. The dogs can be stroked and taken for walks.

After we lost Barkus we decided to create a fish pond in the large back garden. The residents liked the idea and all got involved in digging out the foundations. When complete the moulded pool was set in place. We bought pond plants and a pump to keep the water moving, and – of course – fish. After a report in a local newspaper a local horticulture firm donated more plants and some miniature trees, which they planted for us.

....

People with disabilities have the same sexual urges as non-disabled people. Many living in residential establishments have boyfriends and girlfriends and enjoy kissing and cuddling. This doesn't mean there aren't challenges.

In one home there was young man I will call him Tim, who would upset some of the other residents as he would sit (fully clothed) and masturbate. I and other staff tried to explain to him it was a natural thing but he should do it in his own room. Tim had no problem in understanding what was explained to him, but nonetheless ignored our requests. I arranged for a sex therapist to visit. She chatted to Tim and encouraged him to use a sex toy but obviously only in his bedroom. This solved the problem and saved embarrassment to the other residents.

In another home two Downs young people fell madly in love and wanted to marry, which we did not discourage and along with another member of staff and the bride's sister I arranged their wedding, which was held in a local Church. The couple later moved into a house in the vicinity of the care home, so they could still be supervised as required. Their best man and bridesmaid moved into their home with them.

....

Disabled people are vulnerable and are at heightened risk of abuse, whether sexual, physical, financial or psychological.

Evidence of abuse can be finger marks, multiple bruising, deterioration of health for no apparent reason, weight loss, mood changes, unhappiness about being left alone with a particular person, and an unexplained shortage of money. The abuser might be a family member, a care worker or another resident.

Care must be taken when investigating these apparent signs of abuse. For example I worked with someone who had multiple bruises and we thought initially he was being abused, whereas in fact he had developed an unusual blood condition, which was eventually treated. Another suffered fractures, but ultimately was diagnosed with brittle bone disease.

....

I had to get used to death early in my career. As a young nurse the first death I experienced was a gentleman who had just had an operation and died as he was brought back to the ward. Even though I didn't know him well, the tears just flowed. I was told by a hardened sister: nurse you will get used to this – go and pull yourself together and dry your eyes. In truth, it wasn't something I got used to.

My faith is important to me. I recall Susan, who was severely disabled and began to deteriorate physically. Dying she was admitted to hospital. Along with Sister Eileen – a working nun, whom I discuss in the next chapter – we supported Susan's family. They asked us to visit Susan with them in hospital, which we did. We prayed with them and Susan as she slipped away to be with Jesus.

I remember nursing a close friend of my family who had suffered a severe stroke and lost the ability to speak. Personal things had to be done for him but as a Christian he still loved to read his Bible, which we would position on a pillow for him. He radiated a peace and tranquillity in that ward and without the power of speech was a witness to others. At least two sisters on the ward became Christians through that witness.

The most difficult task for me as a home manager was informing relatives of impending death or that their loved one had died. Sometimes I had to make the decision whether to tell them in the small hours of the morning; had this been their request I had no choice but to do so.

People react in very different ways to death and I would never have told a staff member – as I was told as a young nurse – to 'get used to it'.

Chapter 5:

 The Carers

"He heals the brokenhearted and binds up their wounds."
Psalms 147:3

This book started out as a memoir for family and friends. But as I begin researching and writing I felt it might be of interest to a wider audience. Had this been simply a memoir I would have written it in a straightforwardly chronological way; instead I have chosen to focus on themes. However, since this final chapter is about the kind of people who go into care work, and what motivates them, how I got involved in care work does entail some biography.

As I said at the start of this book I was born in Dublin, moved to England at the age of five, and married a Methodist minister. Looking back I can see that the desire to undertake care work was evident at a young age. When I was quite young my sisters and I would each year travel back from England and stay with various relatives in Dublin. I usually stayed with Aunty Georgette, known as Ninty (when she was born her midwife said "she looks like a lady of ninety"; the name stuck) and Uncle Harry. I loved my holiday there with them. Their bungalow was on a hill overlooking the city. At night I would lay in bed watching the twinkling of the lights of the distant city.

Aunt Ninty and Uncle Harry lived up a long lonely lane off the main country road. Arriving at the bungalow at night Harry had to find matches to light the gas lamp in the hall. There was no electricity or water laid on; the latter came from a well in the back garden. When I think of the lane I can almost smell and taste the wild raspberries, blackberries and strawberries, of which I picked hundreds during those lovely childhood holidays.

I enjoyed collecting the hens' eggs each day, and I also recall watching Harry pointing his shotgun out of the kitchen window at the rabbits. While I abhor cruelty to animals I did acquire a taste for rabbit pie, and I picked fresh mushrooms to go with the pie.

A great enjoyment of these holidays with my aunt and uncle was helping look after my baby cousin Alan. I would assist in bathing him, feeding him, dressing him and rocking him to sleep. One day Ninty suggested I would make a lovely nurse; at eight years of age this ignited a spark that never went out.

During the war – or "state of emergency" as it was called in the South – many men changed their jobs. My father was one such person, and we eventually found ourselves in Northern Ireland. We landed up in Annalong, near Newcastle, County Down. While there, my older sister and I had our first little dog, whom we named Jilly. She was a lovely, but wild, inquisitive, frisky little dog. An example of her inquisitiveness was when my father was cleaning the drains around the bungalow. Jilly sniffed around, not wanting to miss the fun. Unfortunately curiosity got the better of her and she fell head first down the drain. I can still see Dad pulling the little terrier up by his hind legs and giving Jilly a good slap to get the water out of her mouth. After that I watched her every move.

My parents kept a goat in the field next to the bungalow. Mum milked while Dad held the goat's horns as it wriggled and butted. I got upset watching this but loved the milk.

We moved to an old Victorian house in Newcastle, with views of the Mourne Mountains. We couldn't take Jilly or the goat there, which was a big disappointment. However, the arrival of our baby sister provided a new focus of attention. I was four years old when Avril was born and I had to start taking some responsibility, and especially be good for my mother as Dad was now working in England. Because of his absence a friend – May – came to help Mum look after us. I remember May saying to me "you'll be a nurse one of these days because you nurse your dolls so lovingly". That was another spark.

I was forever bandaging my dolls and putting them to bed. About this time I was given a lovely black doll with a beautiful china face. I had many other dolls. I played with these for hours: dressing, undressing, rocking them to sleep, but above all playing hospitals with them.

We all moved to England when Avril was one year old, to live in a big double-fronted house. My parents rented half the house; it was a haven for young children, with big rooms, stables, and fields to play in. We could see horses ploughing the nearby fields.

Mum and Dad later bought a house in a new area of Wolverhampton opposite a bluebell wood. We played in the wood for hours making dens, climbing trees, and acting out Red Indians. My den was always a hospital. I was always the nurse and friends my patients.

While in this house my parents started a Sunday school and church on the estate; the church had been built on the bluebell wood. Through our church connections we were friends with Hugh and Margie, who had a daughter, Kathy, with cerebral palsy (the term then was spastic, a term that has now become pejorative). I befriended Kathy and her parents, who trusted me to babysit so that they could have evenings out. Again Hugh and Margie suggested to me that I train as a nurse.

....

I have already talked about my early experiences in hospitals, but the point I want to make here is that it was evident from an early age that I wanted to work in the caring professionals. Little hints and comments from adults reinforced my sense that I was suited to this kind of work. While people can change their attitudes and interests I think future careers are often evident from an early age. A child who enjoys playing with Lego is probably more like to go into work that involves systems rather than people – which is not to say that he or she can't get on with people. My son recently showed me an on-line quiz which tests the ability to read a person's emotions from a photo simply of their eyes (the 'Mind in the Eyes Test').[3] It was developed by Simon Baron-Cohen, a leading expert on autism. You are asked to choose to decide which emotion – out of four options – is reflected in the eyes. There are thirty-six questions. I scored 33, which is high. A low score doesn't mean that a person is not concerned about others, but simply that he or she is not good at reading emotions and probably wouldn't be suited to working with the kind of people with whom I have worked.

One of the challenges of the care profession in the United Kingdom is that it is underfunded and particularly with elderly care the quality of those employed is variable.

[3] The Mind in the Eyes Test: www.questionwritertracker.com/quiz/61/Z4MK3TKB.html

Some care workers are excellent, but others are doing it because it's the only work available in the local area. While I have worked in some truly happy places I have also had bad experiences. For example, I worked in a home for the elderly in the early 1980s; it was quite challenging. The atmosphere was odd. All the senior staff had to be called by their surname and the officer was known as Matron.

A few years earlier – but in the same town – I had been working at a day centre for people with disabilities run by local social services. On this occasion I was called out on strike. This is the only occasion in my fifty year career where I had to take industrial action. As a union member I felt obliged to participate but I found it very difficult. The dispute did not in fact relate to our part of social services – it arose from children's services – but we all belonged to the same union. The strike lasted two days. I was extremely unhappy about it and vowed I would never do it again. I cannot recall how the dispute was settled, but there is an amusing coda to the story. The director of social services – who happened to be an Anglican clergymen – later caused a stir in the local press by suggesting that one way to reduce the cost of caring for the elderly was to build a portacabin at the end of your garden for your ageing parents.

Ten years later I was working as an assistant officer at a residential home for adults with learning disabilities in South East London. I enjoyed the work with the residents but found the officer in charge very difficult. There was a lack of trust between her and the staff. One day I found she had swapped some of the residents' medication. When I challenged her she said she was only testing whether I noticed the change. This was an extremely dangerous thing to do. I wouldn't want to experience it again.

....

The above are some of my more negative experiences of the caring profession, but I have also experienced some very positive work-places. Some of my best experiences have been with the Catholic Church and its associated charities.

In the late 1970s I worked at a school for young people with dual handicaps in South Buckinghamshire; this is where I acquired my swimming skills discussed in an earlier chapter. A woman who had a big influence on me was Sister Eileen, a mother superior at the local convent. All the nuns at the convent worked, some were midwives and others, such as Eileen, were teachers. Eileen was very down to earth. One day I saw her lying down on the floor in her usual attire of T-shirt and trousers (she didn't wear a habit). One of our students – Simon – was dual-handicapped. He was placed out of his chair and onto the floor so as to give him a different position. He pushed himself by one leg and arm to move himself along the room, in order to experience the difficulties he must have been having. We all tried it ourselves and found it very challenging. What I learnt from Eileen was to try to put yourself in the position of the other person and learn from it.

With experience I acquired more managerial responsibility so that by the late 1980s I had become an officer. Having moved to Sussex I found a post in a home for people with physical disabilities. While I initially started as a care assistant, after about three month I was promoted to Care Officer. The role involved managing relations between care assistants and senior staff. Sometime after, another post became vacant: Assistant Officer in Charge (AOIC). It meant more office-type work and more responsibility. I didn't know whether to apply for it. The Officer in Charge came to me and said I had done a very good job as Care Officer and she wanted me to apply for this new post. I was duly appointed. My experience of being interviewed twice in the same establishment was rather daunting. The role of AOIC involved sleep-ins, which means you are on call if the waking staff need particular help. I thoroughly enjoyed my work there, and it gave me the confidence to apply for a job of similar rank when eventually we moved to the edge of London.

After the unhappy experience of the home where the manager "tested" us by switching drugs I decided to apply for the post of Home Leader (manager) at a residential home for young people with learning difficulties in the Borough of Bexley. I was one of eight interviewees and was delighted to be offered the job. Again, I came into contact with the Catholic Church. First, a little history. The Catholic Handicapped Children's Fellowship was founded in the mid-1960s, and in the 1970s the decision to open a short-stay home to provide respite care for the physically handicapped was taken. It was funded out of a donation from the Order of the Missionary Sisters of the Sacred Heart. Initially the home was established nearer the centre of London – south of the river – and run by the Diocese. After financial difficulties it was taken over by the Catholic Children's Society and moved to outer London.

My time with the Catholic Children's Society was one of the best of my career. I have recounted experiences from there in earlier chapters. The relationship with the local Church – a modern building next to the home – was very positive. What I also enjoyed was the relative autonomy of the job: the ability to come up with and realise ideas, such as the conversion of houses to self-supporting homes, like 'Number 3', which I discussed in an earlier chapter.

The opening ceremony for Number 3 was a great occasion. A lot of planning was involved and much tidying up of the very large garden. We had a marque put up. The residents were involved in arranging the catering for the roughly 100 guests, who included many dignitaries from the Society. My manager put together a very moving dedication service. There was an address by the Catholic bishop and many other priests officiated.

The modern home – which consisted of five large seven-bedroomed detached houses – had replaced a very large institutional home. At the ceremony for Number 3 we had a display of vintage photographs of the old home. Older people recalled seeing these children walking in pairs around the local area.

....

As a manager I often had to interview people and this made me reflect on what makes for a good care worker. A solid general education – basic literacy and numeracy – obviously helped and this would be reflected in their paper application. Other attributes had to be discerned from the interview. The person had to understand the importance of confidentiality. An ability to communicate with people who by their nature often struggled to be understood was essential (hence the importance of being able to "read emotions"). I looked for evidence of having worked in a face-to-face environment. Volunteering was a good sign.

The balance between following procedures and showing initiative was not always an easy one to strike, but the ability to work without close supervision was important. At the same time it was important to be part of a team. Quite obviously, reliability was essential, for as someone once said: half the battle is just turning up for work. Spurious reasons for non-attendance – such as "sickies" – undermined the work of the home.

The willingness to acquire new skills has been essential to my own development and I valued it in others. I have lost count of the courses I have been on over the years, but among them were ones on first aid (renewed every three years), food hygiene, health and safety, staff supervision, and "break-a-way" (a form of self-defence). In retirement I haven't stopped educating myself. I have taken on-line courses, such as one on 'Psychology and Mental Health' (Liverpool University) and another on dementia (University College London). I am currently doing a further course on dementia through Birmingham University.

The core duties of a care assistant are to provide a safe place and to support the clients in practical ways, such as in personal hygiene. The care assistant also has to help with preparing drinks, meals, laundry, washing, ironing, but all the time encouraging the resident or client to be as independent as possible. No two days will be the same.

....

Families can also be carers, as can close friends. Caring can be physical in nature, but need not be, as in the case of a mental disability. You can become a carer without fully realising it. As a society we face the challenge that carers are often not adequately supported, which raises the question: who cares for the carers?

We can't rely on the state. Strong voluntary organisations, such as churches, are essential. There are many specialised support groups, although there are still conditions for which there is no appropriate charity or organisation.

In the early 1980s I started a National Schizophrenic Fellowship (NSF) group. THE NSF has been renamed Rethink, which I think is a better name. We had a family member who suffered a mental breakdown and I felt the need to create a support group for carers in a similar situation. We began with six or seven regulars. There would be visiting speakers and practical advice. The group grew to around twenty. This demonstrated there was a real need for such support in what was an average size town.

Postscript

Have things got better for the disabled since I started work in the late 1950s? On balance, I have to say yes. The UK is a much richer country than in 1958 and so it's possible to spend more on health and social services. On the other hand, we are living longer and the ratio of workers to dependent people has worsened. But perhaps more important than increased wealth has been a change in attitudes and policy. As I have outlined, until the 1970s there was no statutory obligation to educate the disabled and as a result generations of people were incapable of undertaking even the simplest of tasks, such as using public toilets. Along with the new requirement to provide education there was a move to de-institutionalise disability, with the closure of the big hospitals and an emphasis on independent living within the community. This had a negative side, particularly in the area of mental health, but on balance the policy was sound. I hope that in my small way I helped realise this new vision.

Another change for the better was a greater sensitivity in the language used to describe particular kinds of disability; such semantic changes should not be dismissed as "political correctness".

My faith has sustained me, both personally and professionally. And the role of charities – both those with a religious foundation and secular ones – should be acknowledged. Of course, they benefit from state support; in the UK it is ultimately taxpayers who fund social services. Nonetheless, the care sector would have a different ethos without the involvement of these charities.

I hope that readers of this book will be inspired to get involved in working with disabled people and ensuring that the next fifty years see even greater improvements in their care.